The Symbolism of Color

The Symbolism of Color

A Newcastle Classic

by Ellen Conroy

NEWCASTLE PUBLISHING CO., INC.
NORTH HOLLYWOOD, CALIFORNIA

Originally published in 1921 by William Rider & Son, Limited of London.

ISBN: 0-87877-236-7
A Newcastle Classic
First printing 1996
10 9 8 7 6 5 4 3 2 1
Printed in the United States of America.

Cover design © 1996 Michele Lanci-Altomare

Cover illustration © 1996 Damian Valentine Mayek
Illustration dedicated to the memory of Janise Pate

CONTENTS

THE SYMBOLISM OF COLOUR

CHAPTER I

COLOUR A TRUE SYMBOL

"The great below clenched by the great above."—E. B. B.

"GOD made the country; man made the town," says William Cowper, and almost everyone will agree that it is the deprivation of the colour of the country that makes our towns so sadly depressing, for nearly all people appreciate colour, though perhaps in a general way. They realise that colour helps to beautify the world.

Other people, however, look upon colour as one of the greatest joys in life. The colour of the woods, the flowers, the sunrise, and the sunset are sources of the very deepest emotion, exalting them above mere interest in external things into the very highest realms of vision and beauty. The colours of an artist like Titian make them realise the joy of living. Even the word-pictures of the poets do the same, so that they become firm believers in the

1

poetic fallacy that what is beautiful in nature reflects what is beautiful in the mind of man. Thus Buddha watching the sun rise seems to clothe Nature with his own luminous soul, which is striving to make a new age begin on the earth.

Edwin Arnold, in his *Light of Asia*, tells us that the Buddha rose just before the False Dawn and stood—

> " Watching the sleeping earth with ardent eyes
>   And thoughts embracing all its living things;
>   While o'er the waving fields that murmur moves
>   Which is the kiss of Morn waking the lands,
>   And in the East that miracle of Day
>   Gathered and grew. At first a dusk so dim
>   Night seems still unaware of whispered dawn,
>   But soon—before the jungle-cock crows twice—
>   A white verge clear, a widening, brightening white,
>   High as the herald star, which fades in floods
>   Of silver, warming into pale gold, caught
>   By topmost clouds, and flaming on their rims
>   To fervent golden glow, flashed from the brink
>   With saffron, scarlet, crimson, amethyst;
>   Whereat the sky turns splendid to the blue,
>   And, robed in raiment of glad light, the King
>   Of Life and Glory cometh."

As we read the passage the whole scene arises before us, of the lonely watcher and the glorious Eastern sky. In other versions of the same event, whoever, we have more definite teaching concerning these beautiful sunrise hues. The Buddha plays his vina and the colour of the sky changes according to his seven notes—yellow, blue, violet, green, pink, white, and cream; not colours given by chance, but of deep esoteric meaning.

Did we but know it, no doubt the seven strings on the lute of Apollo had once the same significance; and though we know these seven strings had other meanings as well, yet we must not therefore dismiss our theory, for "Is not God able to say many things in one?" That is the whole essence of the understanding of symbolism, that there are planes of interpretation.

There has always existed a belief in the essential connection between colour and sound. That is why in everyday language we say "a colour clashes" or "a colour harmonises"—both terms from the sister art of music. The scientist has now worked out this connection,[1] so that we have the following facts:—

		Vibrations per second.
A tenor voice produces		400
Red light	,,	400,000,000,000,000
A soprano voice	,,	700
Violet light	,,	700,000,000,000,000

Thus light gives a finer vibration than sound to the extent of a million million times, and this is one reason why, when the mind is so tired that even music seems wearisome, it can be healed by means of colour. Professor Wallace Rimington of King's College made a colour organ in which colours were thrown on a screen when the organ was played.

[1] Dr Mount Bleyer of New York invented the vibrograph to give the connection between colour and sound.

Few people recognise that colours are powers, forces, vitalities, and vibrations.[1] Yet such they are, and on the physical plane we are now learning to enlist them in all kinds of occupations, as varied as that of the physician, the gardener, the brewer, and the baker. Every year we are finding out more clearly how we can use these vibrations for the benefit of man. Every year new hospitals are being opened for colour healing. Every year we are finding out how we can obtain better crops by means of the application of coloured rays.[2] The meteorologist[3] has taken up the colour of the sky as an indication of weather, and is making exhaustive tabulation of facts in order to make more definite the lore which we learnt as children in such rhymes as :—

> " Evening red and morning grey
>   Sets the traveller on his way ;
>   Evening grey and morning red
>   Brings down rain upon his head."

When we think of colours and read into them some of the wonderful truths with which they have been associated for many centuries, we are astonished to find that there is a direct correspondence between the value apportioned to a colour on the physical plane and the value given symbolically. Swedenborg was continually insisting that there was no true symbolism without a direct correspondence. Thus, if we take the lions at the base of Nelson's column

[1] See Appendix V.
[2] See Appendix VI.   [3] See Appendix III.

and substitute any other animals, our minds would be instinctively offended. Why? Because Nelson and his men had in them the same quality or qualities that we associate with the lion.

Elizabeth Barrett Browning grips this great truth and expresses it in her poem of *Aurora Leigh* :—

> " Verily I was wrong,
> And verily many thinkers of this age,
> Ay, many Christian teachers, half in heaven,
> Are wrong in just my sense, who understand
> Our natural world too insularly, as if
> No spiritual counterpart completed it,
> Consummating its meaning, rounding all
> To justice and perfection, line by line,
> Form by form, nothing single or alone ;
> The great below clenched by the great above."

CHAPTER II

THE OLD LANGUAGE OF RED

"The Holy Grail, rose-red, with beatings in 't, as if alive."
TENNYSON.

CONSIDERING first the colour red as being the lowest in the spectrum, how is this correspondence manifest? Red is the colour of the blood; hence, is it surprising that red is the colour denoting life and action, cheerfulness and enthusiasm? Red is used by healers as a powerful stimulant and tonic, thus it has the meaning of health and vigour. This is why nearly all red stones are said to have health-giving and disease-preventing properties. The ruby in China and Japan is said to give long life, health, and happiness. All the imperial decrees of China have to be written or printed in red as a sign that there is the power behind to force them to be carried out. Children's clothing must contain some part of red. Usually this consists of a piece of red material twisted together with a pig's-tail, thus making a talisman of great power against sickness.

In India and Persia the garnet is said to bring deep, abiding health to its possessor. The Romans used the red coral as a talisman to protect their children from all manner of diseases; while in India, China, and Japan it is used to-day as a safeguard against cholera. The red carnelian was used by the Hebrews to prevent attacks of plague, and in China it is worn to prevent stomach troubles.

Again, we find the healthy man is inclined to be more cheerful than the sickly man; so we instinctively think of Mr Greatheart as a man with rosy cheeks. The garnet has nearly always been said to bestow the gift of cheerfulness upon its wearer.

Then we find that the healthy man is usually more courageous and daring than the weakling; hence red often means courage. In fact, the lack of red in the face is taken as a sign of the lack of courage—as in *Macbeth*, where the page-boy is told:

> "Go prick thy face and over-red thy fear,
>   Thou lily-livered boy."

Courage was said to be the gift of Mars, the god of war; hence red is the colour of war, whether in its most barbaric, cruel form or in its chivalrous form.

Astrologers assign this colour to the planet Mars from its symbolic value, and not merely because Mars looks red in the heavens. Mr Alan Leo writes thus:

"The planet Mars, which is known by its red colour, is said to be hot and exhaustive in its influence. It presides over all adventure, enterprise, and heroic acts. It makes the mind daring, combative, courageous, fearless, and venturesome. In everything where pluck, force, and energy are required, the Mars man will be foremost. He will be first in any acts of bravery, and often regardless of his life and of the consequences of any noble act where courage is required."

So it is that the brave man is known as the man of self-sacrifice. Thus the colour of red takes on this added meaning of self-sacrifice, sorrow, or suffering, which at first seem contradictory meanings to those of enthusiasm, life, and cheerfulness.

In art the martyrs are often clothed in red as a sign that they have suffered, and also as a sign that they had the enthusiasm for the cause, so that the sorrows and cruelties they endured were accounted by them nothing; for red is pre-eminently the colour of enthusiasm, of the fire which inspires a man to fight his way through all obstacles or perish in the attempt. It is thus most fitting that Moses should receive his life work when near the burning bush, which is surely the most appropriate symbol of the quality necessary before one can become the leader of a nation or change it from one of slaves to one of freemen. Red is the colour of the leader, the colour of the kingly robes.[1] Then we may remember that pretty legend of the Christmas Rose, when the shepherd's little daughter, having no other gift to offer the infant Christ, gave him a fragrant white rose, which was no sooner touched by the Babe than it became a deep glorious red, emblematic of his future suffering.

---

[1] In ancient Wales red robes showed honourable rank.

Red is also the colour of the flame of love. As Robert Burns sings gaily :—

> " Oh, my Love is like a red, red rose,
> That's newly sprung in June."

Perhaps you remember that picture of Rossetti called " Dante's Dream," where Beatrice lies cold and still, clad in white, while Love is seen clothed in rose-red robes leading Dante to her side :—

> " Then Love said, ' Now shall all things be made clear ;
> Come and behold our lady where she lies.' "

Based on very much the same thought there was an old legend that a red carbuncle was placed at the prow of Noah's ark to give light and guidance. This legend no doubt grew out of the appropriateness of red as a symbol for the burning love that directed the boat and brought it safely to Ararat, and also from the fact that the carbuncle gives off a faint phosphorescent glow in the dark. Psychics see this very clearly indeed, but it is visible also to persons of normal vision.

Among nearly all primitive nations red berries, such as those of the mountain ash, symbolise the Spirit of God. They have been called by such names as "holy seed" or " fructifying honey dew."

In front of the high altar of a church or cathedral is seen the red lamp burning perpetually as a sign of the deep, intense, sacrificial, all-enduring love of the Creator.

The communion wine also partakes of this mystic

symbolism, when the joy, the fervour, and the uplift of the spiritual life is imparted to man. There is a beautiful passage in Tennyson's "Holy Grail," when this mystic cup is seen by Sir Percival's sister floating down into her convent cell on a shaft of silver light, making wondrous melody in its passage :—

> " And down the long beam stole the Holy Grail,
> Rose-red with beatings in 't, as if alive,
> Till all the white walls of my cell were dyed
> With rosy colours leaping on the wall ;
> And then the music faded, and the Grail
> Passed, and the beam decayed, and from the walls
> The rosy quiverings died into the night."

Or we may like to call to mind the esoteric order of Rosicrucians, in which all the glorious symbolism of the Rose and the Cross blended.

Or again, we may think of the red carnelian buckle of Isis which was attached to the neck of the deceased while these words were chanted :—

"The blood of Isis, and the strength of Isis, and the words of power of Isis shall be mighty to act as powers to protect this great and divine being, and to guard him from him that would do unto him anything that he holdeth in abomination."

.   .   .   .

You will find that in all symbolism there is an exalted meaning given to the symbol and a debased meaning ; *e.g.* a dog may mean all that is noble and full of devotion, or it may give the meaning of all that is mean, low, and despicable.

In the case of red it may, as we have seen, be the

sign of the sublime, strong love of the Creator; but at the same time it can refer to debased love and carnal passion, *i.e.* love without the sacrificial element. Thus we have in Revelation xvi. 3 "the great red dragon who seeks to destroy the woman clothed with the sun," *i.e.* the woman or soul who is clothed with the Sun of Righteousness. The dragon is frustrated in his attempt by Michael, whose name means "Like unto God," for what is ignoble must ever yield to the noble.

Sometimes red may be used as a sign of exuberant animal spirits, *e.g.* in the expression "to paint the town red."

Lastly, let us remember that the name Adam means red, and so he symbolises man unregenerate, *i.e.* of the earth, earthy.

. . . .

Perhaps it would be wise to consider the colour pink next. Pink is hardly a colour so much as a tint; but as it has a definite symbolism, I have placed it next to red. It is a most useful colour in healing. In the human aura it often denotes the healer. Certainly in its esoteric meaning it denotes the man who wishes to use his life for the healing of others, and the man who receives inspiration how he can help to uplift humanity. Unfortunately, our poets do not often use the word because of its ugly sound.

When Buddha sat under his Bo-tree (*Ficus religiosa*) to meditate how he could save the world, it is said that his whole body became enveloped in

a most radiant blush-rose colour.   Edwin Arnold
describes this scene :—

> " There flew
> High overhead that hour five Holy Ones
> Whose free wings faltered as they passed the tree.
> ' What power superior draws us from our flight ? '
> They asked,—for spirits feel all force divine,
> And know the sacred presence of the pure.
> Then looking downward, they beheld the Buddh
> Crowned with a rose-hued aureole, intent
> On thoughts to save ; while from the grove a voice
> Cried, ' Rishis ! this is he shall help the world.
> Descend and worship.'   So the Bright Ones came
> And sang a song of praise, folding their wings ;
> Then journeyed on, taking good news to God."

The colour pink is said to be the esoteric colour of
the mystic number five, which is the number of
power, inspiration, and love-healing ; *e.g.* five is the
number of points in King Solomon's seal, which was
a talisman of power and inspiration.   The Pool of
Bethesda, we may remember, had five porches, and it
was there that the sick were healed.   We see from
this connection that similar truths are wrapped up
in other groups of symbols.   In fact, we find that
whether we take colours, or numbers, or trees, or
animals, or mountains, or rivers, we learn the same
deep truths.   The mystics knew that each was an
expression of the heavenly mind :—

> " Earth's crammed with heaven
>   And every common bush afire with God,
>   But only he who sees takes off his shoes." [1]

[1] E. B. B., *Aurora Leigh.*

Carlyle used pink in its debased sense when he speaks "of the rose-pink hue of sentimentality," meaning a hue that lacks full virility.

.   .   .   .

When we come to the colour orange, however, we find that the ancients hardly ever refer to it. If it had very much red in it, it came under the symbolism of red. If it had very much yellow in it, then the symbolism of yellow was considered to embrace it. They did not know it as a primary colour.

CHAPTER III

THE OLD LANGUAGE OF YELLOW

"Into the yellow of the Rose Eternal . . .
Me Beatrice drew."—DANTE.

YELLOW is one of the most interesting colours. Being the colour of the sun, all the attributes of the sun were given to it.

Like red it was considered a masculine colour, while green, blue, and violet were thought of as feminine. Like red, too, it is used by healers as a tonic. As it is of such healing value to the brain, we are not surprised to find that amber has been used as an antidote to insanity. Yellow stones are said to bring happiness to their owners, for yellow was said to be the colour of unity—unity in affection, unity with the spiritual powers of the universe, unity with the Sun of Righteousness who comes with healing in his wings.

This old meaning of the colour yellow was well known and understood in the old Roman Catholic Church. Therefore Dante, who wrote much of his great *Divine Comedy* consciously or unconsciously to interpret these old ideas and to enshrine them in

14

poetry for evermore, says when he has reached the
highest part of heaven and is once more with
Beatrice :—

> "Into the yellow of the Rose Eternal . . .
> Me Beatrice drew."

The Pope (on the fourth Sunday in Lent) presents
a golden rose of jewels to any person greatly beloved
by the Church.

One can notice in the world at present a deep and
increasing love for all yellow colours,[1] for it is a colour
that gives the appearance of sunlight to the most
cheerless rooms.   May we not also hope that it is a
sign that the world is now striving after unity, and
the desire to understand the other person's point
of view ?

The yellow robe donned by the Buddhist is a
symbol that he is now on the path that is to lead
to spirituality.   The *Light of Asia* tells us that
Buddha taught his supreme truths "to his own, them
of the yellow robe."   He taught them to practise
"yoga."   What is "yoga"?   To the Western mind
it usually means a kind of magic—even charlatanism,
but the real meaning of the word is "union."   The
belief of these yellow-robed men is that they have
within them a spark of the Godhead, and that, by
suppressing the bodily desires and by concentrating
their whole mental and psychic energies towards
trying to understand this higher part of their nature,

[1] See Appendix IV.

they will become united with the Supreme Spirit and will understand how to do many things and see many things that the ordinary man cannot do or see.

Vishnu is clad in yellow for the same reason. In the vision of Ezekiel, God is seen in the colour amber; at least, the amber colour is the outward sign of the presence of God.

In the ceremony of making a child become a Brahmin a piece of saffron cloth is bound to his arm with a yellow cord. The Mexicans gave the name Kan to the god who supported the sky. The same word meant yellow.

Yellow is the royal colour of China, and the privilege of wearing yellow is most jealously guarded, for does it not show that its possessor is a Son of the Sun? Similarly the saffron robes of the ancient Irish nobility were a sign of their rank.

Yellow is the marriage colour in India, and the bride stains her hands yellow as a sign of the happiness and unity she expects in her married life. The Roman bride wore a crocus-coloured veil and yellow shoes. Among the Jews marriage may be performed under the Talis, an orange silk robe stretched on four posts. The bride and her maids walk round it seven times, which is said to be in memory of the siege of Jericho.

It might also be noted, in Calderon's picture of Ruth and Naomi, that Ruth, who wishes ever to be with Naomi, wears a yellow robe—perhaps by chance, perhaps by design, or perhaps by intuition.

Among the Mayas and Egyptians the great serpent of the universe (who symbolises Eternity and Wisdom) was said to be blue in colour but to have yellow scales. In China the golden cock proclaims the dawn. The golden hawk, the golden eagle, the golden ass,[1] and the golden calf were all symbols of deity. Athena, who represented union with the mind of Zeus, had a robe called the "peplus," a crocus-coloured garment with figures woven into it of the gods conquering the giants. It was suspended to the mast of a ship when it was to be carried in procession, being too holy to be carried by hands.

The mundane egg which is to be met with in nearly all ancient religions, whether of India, Egypt, Phœnicia, Japan, or the South Sea Islands, was said to have been a golden one—that is, it represents the sun or deity. Probably our children's tale of the goose that lays the golden eggs is a survival of one of these ancient beliefs.

We must remember, too, that the colour of gold not only partook of the meaning of the colour yellow, but also of the symbolism of the metal gold, which is the metal of the sun. Thus the colour began to mean all that was pure, all that had been refined, and hence glory and wisdom. Thus the halo of saints and of God is often made of gold leaf. Similarly

---

[1] Read the *Golden Ass* of Apuleius, where the hero only regains his real shape by eating roses, which are symbols of prayer.

2

the gates and doors of heaven are nearly always represented as being of gold.

We may remember, too, that among the emblems attached to St John are the eagle and the River Pison. This River Pison is mentioned in Genesis as flowing through Havilah, where there is much gold. It therefore became the river of inspiration and the wisdom of God; and since St John received the greatest vision, it was considered his most appropriate emblem.

The ladder which Jacob saw in his dream at Bethel or the House of God is described by Dante as being of gold:—

> " I saw reared up,
> In colour like to sun-illumined gold,
> A ladder, which my ken pursued in vain,
> So lofty was the summit."

For it is by the ladder of wisdom that we attain wisdom and receive inspiration.

The Pre-Raphaelite Brotherhood made it their particular joy to replace this beautiful symbolism into art. Thus Dante Gabriel Rossetti speaks very beautifully in "The Blessed Damozel" of a golden thread of life that is woven into the robes of the spirits who arrive in the next world after having lived during earth life in unity with God:—

> " We two, she said, will seek the groves
> Where the Lady Mary is,
> With her five handmaidens, whose names
> Are five great symphonies :—

> Cecily, Gertrude, Magdalen,
>> Margaret and Rosalys.
> Circle-wise sit they with bound locks
>> And bosoms covered,
>> Weaving the golden thread
> To fashion the birth-robes for them
>> Who are just born, being dead."

This golden thread is spoken of by the mystic Blake:—

> "I give you the end of a golden string,
>> Only wind it into a ball;
> It will lead you in at heaven's gate,
>> Built in Jerusalem's wall."

The Greeks also had a legend of a golden thread by which Jupiter drew up souls to heaven. Here we might mention the Golden Bough given to Æneas in order that he may visit the dead and yet retain his life (*Æneid*, bk. vi. 29).

In the Kalevala, the great Finnish epic, Ilmater is invoked:—

> "Ancient daughter of Creation,
>> Come in all thy golden beauty."

And as Ilmater stands for wisdom, we are not surprised that Ecclesiasticus should say, "Get wisdom, and get much gold by her." So also Keats writes:—

> "Much have I travelled in the realms of gold."

In Babbit's book on colour there is an illustration of the aura seen round the head of a man. Above the top part of the head is seen the colour yellow. Now, the phrenologist locates this as the seat of spirituality; thus we see that once more two studies agree in their conclusions. Yellow was thus to the ancients the greatest of all the colours, and had the most exalted meaning.

It is perhaps to be expected, then, that in its degraded meaning it is the saddest of all colours, for we recognise the deceitful Judas very often in ancient pictures from the fact that he is given dingy yellow robes. The Jews in Venice formerly had to wear yellow hats, to show the scorn in which the Venetians held them. Yellow is the colour of decaying vegetable life, of the poorness of life. Thus it means separation instead of unity.

CHAPTER IV

THE OLD LANGUAGE OF GREEN

"Hope rules a land for ever green."—WORDSWORTH.

"HOPE rules a land for ever green," says Wordsworth. He means a land where nothing dies, for green is the colour of plant life, the colour of spring and of all that is fresh and young and joyous.

When looking at Watts' picture of Hope, we see that she sits almost like a picture of Despair, but she is trying to obtain music from her one last string. We notice that the green Watts uses is of a particularly hard, bluish character, so unlike the joyous green of spring. When Rossetti in "Dante's Dream" depicts the two maidens lifting the veil from the face of Beatrice, we notice what a full rich green he uses for their robes, for he wishes to make his colour proclaim the fact that he feels no despair, but a sublime Hope and Faith which will go with him until the time that Beatrice will draw him into the "yellow of the Rose Eternal."

Shelley understood that green meant hope and gladness, for he wrote:—

> "Many a green isle needs must be
> In the deep, wide sea of Misery,

> Or the mariner worn and wan
> Never thus could journey on
> Day and night, and night and day,
> Drifting on his weary way,
> With the solid darkness black
> Closing round his vessel's track :
> Whilst above, the sunless sky
> Big with clouds hangs heavily ;
> And behind, the tempest fleet,
> Hurries on with lightning feet,
> Riving sail, and cord, and plank,
> Till the ship has almost drank
> Death from the o'er-brimming deep,
> And sinks down, down, like that sleep
> When the dreamer seems to be
> Weltering through eternity."

Among the ancient Druids of Wales, green was the colour of the robes of the "ovates," that is, the men who were hoping to become bards or Druids later.

The colour green was used by the people of the East with a much deeper significance, however. The Hindoos said that Om, the Sun, drove across the sky in a chariot drawn by a green horse with seven heads, and preceded by Aruna, the Dawn. As we have no green horses in nature, the statement must be highly symbolic. Horses are always a sign of knowledge.[1] In the old Hindoo zodiacs, instead of the constellation Aries or the Ram,

---

[1] *Cf.* Sanskrit "harit"=(1) a horse, (2) the light, bright, shining. *Cf.* Pegasus, the winged horse of the Muses, in poetical imagination.

we often have a horse. Aries is the sign governing the head or mentality. The horse is used
in exactly the same way. The number seven
means what is complete in both body and spirit,
for it contains the basic four (which is the number
of man, who has to perfect his fourfold nature—
body, mind, soul, and spirit), and also it contains
the three, which is the perfection of the Trinity,
for every great religion has contained a Trinity.
Thus we see that seven refers to perfection in all
things, whether of heaven or of earth. What, then,
do we mean by a seven-headed *green* horse? This
—that the knowledge and wisdom of Om are eternal,
everlasting, all-enduring, and that they comprehend
the whole universe.

In Palestine St George is sometimes called "the
everlasting green one," for the fight between good
and evil is never-ending, but to the true St George
the victory is ever assured.

Time was addressed by the Egyptians as the
"everlasting green one," for the main experiences
of life are the same to everyone, whether born
now or hundreds of years ago. External circumstances alter, but each person has the same lessons
to learn. The Fortunate Isles of the Greeks and
the Islands of the Blessed of the North American
Indians are said to have been green. Nearly all
evergreen plants were considered especially sacred.
Edgar Allan Poe addressed his love as

" A green isle in the sea."

The Hindoos say that the emerald gives the gift
of knowledge and memory. It also gives the ability
to tell the future, even as the green laurel tree of
Apollo did. The emerald also confers immortality
on the soul, and enables it to gain faith. This belief
will surely explain why greenstone amulets are so
common in the tombs of the Egyptians, for faith
would bring them safely to the Fields of Peace,
where immortality was enjoyed.

Isis, the goddess of the crescent moon, which often
mystically means the pure soul, is sometimes called
the "Lady of the Emerald"—that is, she whose
soul is pure enough to gain immortality.

When Pizarro went to Mexico he found that a
goddess there was worshipped as the Goddess of
the Emerald.

The emerald is often seen on the breastplates of
Pallas and of Minerva, for both these goddesses
stand for the Divine mind—the all-enduring Wisdom.
The Virgin Mary is often represented clothed in a
green mantle and standing on the crescent moon.
She has faith and hope until the Day-star awakes
in her heart. The walls of the New Jerusalem are
seen by John in Revelation to be made of jasper.
The New Jerusalem, like the Ark and the Temple,
is said by mystics to be a soul symbol; hence, how
appropriate that the green jasper should be the
material of which it is said to be made! Among
the Chinese, Tao is said to have been miraculously
born of "the excellent Virgin of Jasper."

Green is sometimes said to be the colour of the planet Mercury,[1] which is the planet governing the mind and conferring knowledge — knowledge not only of the kind essential to material success, but also inspirational knowledge and celestial wisdom. The god Mercury had assigned to him nearly all the main attributes of Hermes, just as Hermes in the same way received the main characteristics of Thot and his companion Anubis. The "green hill of Anubis," where the good souls were directed, is the hill of everlasting life and of Eternal Wisdom. Thot also had green hills dedicated to him. It is probably due to the Phœnicians that we have place names perpetuating this fact, *e.g.* Toot's Hill in Epping Forest, Tothill Street, Tooting, and Tewkesbury. In Christian times the archangel Michael was given the work and attributes of these gods; and surely it is marvellous the number of hills and rocks sacred to St Michael, while in ancient pictures we often see him conducting the souls of the departed to the green hill of Zion.

When we think of the great gifts symbolised by green, how full of meaning seems the green turban of the Mohammedan who has visited Mecca! We can also realise what great truths could have been taught, and no doubt were, in the "Green Schools"[2] of the Persian sufis.

.   .   .   .

Green in its degraded sense gives us "the green-

<hr />

[1] See Appendix II.   [2] See Appendix I.

eyed monster jealousy," which is the direct opposite
of celestial wisdom, for jealousy is always due to
the intrusion of the desires of the self, while celestial
wisdom wishes to give rather than to receive. The
colour green is often said to forebode death. This
idea may be a survival of the ancient worship of
Mercury, and even of St Michael [1] in Christian times,
both of whom were messengers of death.

[1] See picture of St Michael presenting taper of death to the
Virgin (Fra Filippo Lippi).

CHAPTER V

"Blue, 'tis the colour of heaven!"—KEATS.

IN the spectrum we ought to be able to recognise both blue and indigo, though many people find difficulty in recognising the indigo ray. Blue belongs to the cooling end of the spectrum, and thus it is right and fitting that symbolically it should be the colour of Truth, which is the result of calm reflection and never of heated argument. Even in everyday language we speak of "true-blue."

Blue is the colour of the heavens—that is, blue is the colour of the abode of God :—

"Then went up Moses, and Aaron, and Nadab, and Abihu, and seventy of the elders of Israel ; and they saw the God of Israel : and there was under his feet as it were a paved work of sapphire stone, and as it were the very heaven for clearness." [1]

Ezekiel has very much the same vision, not because he copied from an older version, but because it is given to every great seer to realise for himself any real basic truth, such as that God dwells in Truth. Clairvoyant visions often repeat themselves

[1] Exodus xxiv. 9–11.

to different people in different countries and in different ages.

" And above the firmament that was over their heads was the likeness of a throne, as the appearance of a sapphire stone : and upon the likeness of the throne was the likeness as the appearance of a man above upon it. And I saw as the colour of amber." [1]

A wonderful vision truly that within Truth dwells the amber of unity and the divine Spirit.

The Egyptian judges wore a breastplate of blue covered with symbolic figures. The blue was to show that they would reverence truth in their judgments and not stoop to bribery.

Moses was commanded to make the robe of the ephod of blue, and on the skirts of it were to be pomegranates of blue. This was to symbolise that the true priest of God was to abound in Truth—not in mere facts and formalities. Truth is ever greater than mere facts. Facts may sometimes give the appearance of an untruth, but Truth is ever one and indivisible. As said previously, it contains unity.

Again Moses was commanded to—

" Speak unto the children of Israel, and bid them that they make them fringes in the borders of their garments, throughout their generations, and that they put upon the fringe of the borders a ribband of blue . . . that ye may remember, and do all my commandments, and be holy unto your God." [2]

Here we might mention that the Rabbins considered that blue was the colour of the two stones on which

[1] Ezekiel i. 26.   [2] Numbers xv. 38.

the Commandments were written.   Plato tells us that the robes of the priests of Atlantis were blue.

The Buddhists say, " Sapphire produces peace of mind and equanimity.   It chases out evil thoughts by establishing healthy circulation.   It opens barred doors to the spirit.   It produces a desire for prayer. It brings peace, but he who would wear it must lead a pure and holy life."

Surely, if all this is true, it is almost essential that we should follow the advice of colour healers and have our ceilings always of blue.

Blue is often called the colour of devotion, but we must remember that devotion is not an end in itself; it is the striving after eternal Truth and Wisdom that matters.

So much did the Hindoos think of the colour that their gods are addressed by the epithet " narayan," and they are said to be born of the sea which ever reflects the blue of heaven.   In Egypt the gods were often painted blue to show their heavenly origin; e.g. Kneph the Creator, the great Mind, wears blue robes. Mummies were shrouded in blue beads to show that they were united with the soul of Truth.

Odin, the wise All-Father of the Scandinavians, is nearly always spoken of as wearing blue robes.   The blue pines near the homes of Philemon and Baucis were sacred to Jupiter.   Sin, the Assyrian god, is said to have had a blue beard.   Our conception of blue beard has taken on the debased meaning of cruelty.

Isis is often called the Lady of the Turquoise, while Osiris is god of the turquoise and the lapis lazuli. The Virgin Mary is often clad in a blue robe, for the same reason that she is often represented as standing by the Well of Truth, as in Arthur Hacker's "Annunciation." The Hindoo Mariama is addressed as "Holy Nari Mariama, mother of perpetual fecundity."

In both Mexico and Chaldea blue was worn as mourning, being a token of the joy that the soul realised in the Fields of Peace.

The turquoise and the lapis lazuli seem to have had in them the two blues that appealed most to the ancients. In the "Burden of Isis" we have these words in praise of Osiris, who is identified with the spirit of the departed :—

"With turquoise is thy hair twined, and with lapis lazuli, the finest of lapis lazuli. Lo, the lapis lazuli is above thy hair."

There is another similar incantation in the Festival Songs of Isis and Nephthys :—

"Thy hair is like turquoise as thou comest from the Fields of Turquoise ; thy hair is like unto the finest of lapis lazuli, and thou thyself art more blue than thy hair. Thy skin and body are like southern alabaster, and thy bones are of silver. The perfume of thy hair is like unto new myrrh, and thy skull is of lapis lazuli."

Since hair is not blue, the statement must be symbolic, and means that the spirit of the departed has now become one with Eternal Truth.

Surely we cannot read the above passages without thinking of the Song of Solomon, where the bridegroom is compared to " bright ivory overlaid with sapphires."

There is another such song in praise of Amen-Ra :—

" Praise to Amen-Ra,
  To the bull of Heliopolis, to the chief of all the gods,
  To the beautiful and beloved god,
  Who giveth life by all manner of warmth,
  By all manner of fair cattle.

  .   .   .   .

  Amen, bull fair of face,
  Beloved in Thebes ;
  He fashioneth earth, the silver and the gold,
  Real lapis lazuli for those who love him."

The same imagery is used by the Buddhists. When Buddha sat under the Bo-tree on his throne of knowledge, all truths were revealed to him. To symbolise this we are told that he saw the great white cosmic umbrella, and also the Fields of Lapis Lazuli, where all the preceding Buddhas dwelt in ecstasy :—

    " He hath o'erthrown the flag of pride,
      He hath obtained the triple knowledge.

      .   .   .   .

      The King of Physicians
      With his heavenly Amrita [1]
      Will dull all human pain
      And lead all flesh to Nirvana.
      Having entered the City of Omniscience,
      And become one with the Buddhas,
      He is now indivisible."

---

[1] Amrita, bread of life.

This last word gives us the key to the whole situation that in the Fields of Lapis Lazuli there dwell the pure spirits who have become the soul of Truth, inseparable from Divine Truth, indivisible from the Spirit of God.

When we consider the Greeks we remember that Homer always speaks of Pallas, the Goddess of Wisdom, as " the blue-eyed maid," for is she not the goddess who teaches the will of Zeus and the truths of Zeus? The heroine of almost every fairy tale in the world is blue-eyed, as a sign that she is the true, good, and lovable maiden who is the object and reward of the quest and labour of the prince.

In the epic of the Finns, Ilmater is invoked in these words :—

> " Rise up, O water-mother,
>   Raise thy blue cap from the billows."

And this makes us think of Venus rising from the blue ocean.

We must recollect that blue was the colour of the robes of the Druidic bards. The bards were men who had been " ovates " and had worn the green. They were still to retain in themselves all that was meant by the green, but blue is symbolically a higher colour, even as it is physically.

Many people think that red would have been a better colour for the bards, because this symbolises the enthusiasm that is so necessary in song and poetry; but the bards were to have more than enthusiasm—they were to have the gift of looking beyond the world and of obtaining great Truths to uplift humanity. They were to be Masters of Wisdom. They were to get beyond mere passion and look into the cooler, calmer regions beyond, whence they could draw these great and deep truths. It makes us think instinctively of Wordsworth's definition of poetry as " Passion recollected in tranquillity."

From the great Triads of the Druids we learn the duties of the bards :—

1. To make a country habitable.

2. To civilise the people.

3. To promote science.

Blake had the same belief in the duty of a poet, which he expresses very beautifully :—

> " I will not cease from mental strife
>   Nor shall my sword sleep in my hand
> Till we have built Jerusalem
>   In England's green and pleasant land."

The work and duty, as given in the first two parts of the Triad, recalls J. Russell Lowell's wonderful lines :—

> " He who would be the tongue of this wide world
> Must string his harp with cords of banded iron
> And strike it with a toil-embrownèd hand."

In our own time, Maurice Maeterlinck has written a little play called *The Blue Bird*. The playbills tell us that the quest of the Blue Bird is the quest for happiness, but it seems to be far more than this. A

bird often symbolises spirit. Thus the quest of the
Blue Bird is really the quest for spiritual truths.[1]
The children in their journey first appeal to their
dead grandparents for the bird. By this Maeterlinck
means us to ask ourselves whether the past was able
to know Truth, and the fact that the children do not
find the bird there shows us that Maeterlinck thinks
Truth is of the future.

Still, the children have grown by appealing to the
past, as is shown when the grandparents measure the
children against the door. They have also another
great fact to learn—that there are no dead.

Next the children ask the Trees if they have the
Blue Bird. These Trees, who think they are the
rightful custodians of the Blue Bird, and resent the
intrusion of the children, represent the persecuting
churches of the world who have become stereotyped
and hate progress. So the children are in great
danger and are only saved when the dog (or human
common sense) bursts his bonds and Fairy Light comes
to the rescue.

The children never find the Blue Bird, for is it
possible to obtain universal Truth and put it in a
cage ? When a man says vaingloriously that he has
all Truth, it is a sign that he is very far from his
statement. Still Mytyl and Tyltyl are better children
for going on their journey, showing that it is the quest
that is the great thing.

.   .   .   .

[1] See Henry Rose, *The Blue Bird.*

Blue in its lowest meaning signifies depression and despair. We have such expressions as "a fit of the blues." Or again it may mean hardness, coldness, or cruelty, even, as in such an expression as "steel-blue eyes" or "Bluebeard." A blue-stocking means someone who has cultivated intellect and left out affection.

CHAPTER VI

"And they put upon him a robe of purple."—ST JOHN.

THE next and highest colour of the spectrum is violet. Like green and blue, it is calming and soothing in its influence. Like green and blue, it is said by the mystics to be a feminine colour. It seems as though the ancient people used the term purple to include violet, and in fact any tint made up of blue and red in whatever proportions. Pliny tells us that the colour of the amaranth is a far more beautiful purple that any the dyers can obtain. This, however, does not help us much, for the amaranth can be almost any shade from red to blue. Even to-day we see how carelessly the word purple is used when we have in a great writer's book the phrase, "the purple rainbow."

The symbolism of purple partakes of the Red of Love and Self-sacrifice and the blue of Truth; hence it was considered symbolic of Wisdom, and is mentioned as being the colour of the canopy [1] of Solomon's chariot. Purple was considered the most glorious of

[1] Song of Solomon iii. 10.

colours, for the purple dye was so costly that it became part of the insignia of royalty. In England it is used as the sign of royal mourning.

Before we really comprehend the symbolism of purple, however, we must reflect that purple was said by the Egyptians to be the colour of the earth. At evening, in some parts of the world, looking across the ploughed fields that seem so red in the daylight, we see that they appear tinged with purple. Our painters of landscape show this purple colour, while our poets speak of purple shadows.

Thus the colour became symbolic of the basic qualities in our nature that form a sure foundation on which to build the very highest qualities—patience, endurance, perseverance, ability to be long suffering and slow to anger. All these qualities are a *sine qua non* to the evolved soul. This is why the suffering Christ was given a purple robe before His crucifixion. It is to show that the King of kings is also the lowliest and most gentle of all beings—that He had such humility as was expressed in the washing of the disciples' feet. As He Himself said: "He who would be the chief among you, let him be your servant." How we think here of the humble, fragrant violet.

We remember the story of Sir Gareth in the *Idylls of the King*.

> " And Gareth bowed himself
> With all obedience to the king, and wrought
> All kind of service with a noble ease
> That graced the lowest act in doing it."

The Egyptians often made their soldiers talismans of amethyst because they said that this stone could give them the necessary calmness of mind to ensure victory. The Magi of Persia said that amethyst was born of the Sun and of the Moon, which confirms us in the belief that purple has all the symbolism of the red and of the blue, the masculine and feminine forces, the spirit and the soul. It evidently seems to have been used in this way by the Finns, for in the "Kalevala," Wainomoinem sails over the "blue back of the waters" till he "gains the purple-coloured harbour" of the next world. Here purple is used of a greater realm than that of the ocean.

Many old rosaries were made of amethyst, because its effect was to make the wearer withdraw from all the trials of the world and worship in a holy calm.

In King's *Ancient Gnostic Gems* we are given a translation of a poem by Marbodus :—

> "On high the amethyst is set
>   In colour like the violet,
>   With flames as if of gold it shows
>   And far it purple radiance throws ;
>   The humble heart it signifies
>   Of him, who in the Saviour dies."

So we see why the martyrs are often represented as being clad in purple. This ability to endure for the truth brings them the fullest reward in the love of the Saviour.

When we see the angels with purple robes it signifies that they partake of the sorrows of Christ and desire to help men with loving messages to attain the heavenly home beyond the blue firmament. In some of the ancient orders of nuns the women wore purple veils as a sign of repentance and of faith in the divine love of God.

Shakespeare, in *A Midsummer Night's Dream*, speaks of the

> "Flower of purple dye
> Hit with Cupid's archery"

—a flower that we now consider to be the pansy, the name of which is probably derived from "Pensez à moi," and emblematic of humility and sweet, loving thoughts.

.   .   .   .

Purple in its debased meaning gives us overweening pride, pomp, and vanity. It is the colour of the rich man who has no love in his heart for Lazarus, and no belief in anything but the things of the world.

CHAPTER VII

THE OLD LANGUAGE OF WHITE

"Oh! what a power has white simplicity."—KEATS.

IT is to be remembered in studying ancient colour symbolism that it was not realised that white was the sum of the seven colours of the rainbow. To us, because we know this fact, white is more naturally the colour of unity than yellow. Thus Shelley writes:—

> "Life like a dome of many-coloured glass
>   Stains the white radiance of eternity."

White, in fact, symbolised not so much unity as purity, innocence, and the great joy of the man who has fought the good fight and attained the spiritual life. It is to symbolise this joy that the souls of the Redeemed in Revelation are clad in white robes. For the same reason Dante sees the souls of the blessed in Paradise in form of a white rose:—

> "In form then of a white rose
>   Displayed itself to me the saintly host
>   Whom Christ in His own blood had made His bride;
>   Faces had they all of living flame,
>   And wings of gold, and all the rest so white,
>   No snow unto that beauty can attain."

40

Tennyson, in "St Agnes' Eve," uses white in the same way to convey the ecstasy of St Agnes:—

> "Make Thou my spirit pure and clear
>   As are the frosty skies,
>   Or this first snowdrop of the year
>   That in my bosom lies."

The Archangel Gabriel is usually known in pictures from the fact that his emblem is the lily—sometimes called the "lily of the annunciation," as a sign that a pure soul is necessary before Christ can take possession of it. Gabriel is usually said to be the Angel of the Moon, to which the colour white and the metal silver were given by astrologers and mystics.

It was the custom of Roman ladies to wear white. The wearing of bright colours was looked upon as portraying a lack of virtue. The word "candidate" tells us that integrity was expected of all persons desiring office.

Hesiod the poet sees Modesty and Justice in white robes:—

> "And those fair forms in snowy raiment bright
>   Leave the broad earth, and heavenward soar from sight;
>   Justice and Modesty, from mortals driven,
>   Rise to th' immortal family of heaven."

Hermas sees the Church as a virgin in white:—

> "Behold there met me a certain virgin, well-adorned, and as if she had just come out of her bride-chamber—all in white, having on white shoes, and a veil down her face, and her head covered with shining hair. Now, I knew by my former visions that it was the church."

The Japanese use white as symbol of death, and a bride wears white as her parents consider her dead to them and belonging only to her husband.

In Revelation there is a curious statement: "To him that overcometh will I give the white stone." It was the custom to give the victor in the games a white stone, so that the sentence seems a truism, as "To him that overcometh will I give the sign of victory"; but when we dig more deeply into the meaning of the white stone we find that it is a sign of deity, of the Spirit of God marking out His chosen one. In the Amaravati tope at the British Museum Buddha is seen sitting on the white stone, and sometimes the white stone is used in place of Buddha. In Ireland, until recent times, white stones were placed in a coffin and called "God's stones." Hence "To him that overcometh will I give the white stone" means that to the victor shall be given the joy of the presence of God, the joy of harmony, the music of the spheres—

> "When the morning stars sang together,
>   And all the sons of God shouted for joy."

There was a similar idea among the Egyptians. In the papyrus of Ani you will note that when he is justified he is shown with white hair. Similarly, Christ in Revelation has hair [1] as white as wool.

In Revelation Christ rides on the white horse. St George is nearly always depicted on a white horse. Castor and Pollux were said to ride on

---

[1] Revelation i. 14.

white horses. A horse, as I have said before, means knowledge. Thus to ride on the white horse means to have all heavenly counsel to aid you in gaining the victory and in obtaining the reward. It is said that there will be one more incarnation of Vishnu, when he will carry the sword of justice and ride the white horse, like Christ in Revelation. We must remember that the horse was used by the Hindoos instead of the Ram. Now as Aries or the Ram is the constellation in which the sun starts his zodiacal journey each year, the ram or horse means the opener of new thought, the dawn of a new era. Hence to ride the white horse means to begin a new kingdom on earth of joy and happiness and purity. When Mahomet comes again he will ride the white horse Alborac. In ancient Rome the white horse was sacred to Jupiter, and once a year the consul, clad in white robes, rode to the Capitol to adore Jupiter as the Sun-god.

Buddha is said to have been borne to earth on a white elephant, *i.e.* on Divine Wisdom or the Holy Ghost. In some of the old Buddhist zodiacs the elephant takes the place of the sign Capricorn or the goat. Capricorn is the sign governing from 21st December to 19th January, and this is the time during which all world-saviours are said to have been born.

Osiris and Zeus are spoken of as white bulls, for the bull betokens cosmic energy and creative force. When Yasôdhara dreams that Siddartha or Buddha is escaping from the palace, she sees "a white bull with wide branching horns."

The Druids proper of Wales wore white robes. It may be mentioned that it took twenty years to train a Druid, so that surely the white robe in their case was a sign that the wearer had laboured much and conquered many things. The work of a Druid is given in the Triads :—

1. To keep his word.
2. To keep his secret.
3. To keep the peace.

It must be remembered that he was a bard previous to being a Druid. Druidship was the last stage of initiation, and what he learnt in this was not to be given out directly to the world but to be expressed only in the inward power that accrued to him. He kept the peace because he knew that the arts flourish in times of peace and are destroyed during war. Still we must remember that when war came he was ever ready to lead the people, and many a Druid died in the forefront of the battle, for to him death was the gate of life and the entrance to the joy of the Mighty Hu.

The symbolism of silver is related to that of white, for silver is the colour of the moon, of chastity, and the ability to radiate purity and joy, however dark the night and difficult the circumstances. Artemis and Diana are both virgin goddesses of the moon, punishing evil deeds and immorality.

Solomon speaks of the "silver cord." It is the

bond between the mortal and the everlasting : when it is loosed then the soul is released and regains the music of the spheres.

Sir Walter Raleigh writes :—

> " My soul like quiet palmer
>   Travelleth toward the land of heaven,
>   Over the silver mountains
>   Whence spring the nectar fountains."

In the Paradise of the Brahmins, Brahma has his being in the heart of a silver rose (Tamura Pua); that is, in the heart of all fragrance, sweetness, beauty, purity, and joy there is God.

.   .   .   .

In its opposite symbolism white means lack of courage and sometimes deceitfulness—*e.g.* " whited sepulchres."

CHAPTER VIII

"Upon all the glory shall be a defence."—Isaiah.

ALTHOUGH science does not now consider black as a colour, yet it is still considered so by the public and was considered so by the ancients. To them it was the colour of mystery and of the mysterious ways and wisdom of God.

In Egypt, Kneph the Creative Mind was sometimes addressed as "Thrice unknown darkness transcending all intellectual perception," for certainly the wisdom of God is beyond the comprehension of human intellect. One of our modern mystics, Henry Vaughan, seems to arrive at the same thought when he says, "There is in God a deep and dazzling darkness"; meaning that the mysteries of God are unfathomable but glorious. Black was considered the colour of wisdom, and Milton, who is so accurate in his symbolism, uses it as such :—

> "Goddess staid and holy,
> Whose saintly visage is too bright
> To hit the sense of human sight;
> And therefore to our weaker view
> O'erlaid with black, staid wisdom's hue."

46

Black also symbolised eternity; thus Night, the mother of all things, was sometimes portrayed by the Greeks in a starry veil, holding two children—one white and the other black—to symbolise Time and Eternity. Osiris and also Horus are sometimes painted white and sometimes black, to show that they manifested themselves in time though they were eternal.

Black also meant silence—the things that are not to be revealed to everyone—the thoughts that lie too deep for tears—the innermost and most sacred experiences of life. It is not that we ought to be selfish with our knowledge—far otherwise :—

> "Give all thou canst; high heaven rejects the lore
> Of nicely-calculated less or more." [1]

It is that certain experiences can only be comprehended by a person having similar experiences. In olden times a black rose was used as the symbol of the silence of an initiate, such a silence as that comprehended by St Paul when speaking of the man who was caught up into heaven and heard [2] unspeakable things which it is not lawful for any man to utter. The great promise [3] to every initiate is, "I will give thee the treasures of darkness."

As the old proverb says, "If you would know more you must be more." Until then there is a veil [4]

---

[1] Wordsworth, "Within King's College Chapel."
[2] 2 Corinthians xii. 4.   [3] Isaiah xlv. 3.
[4] Exodus xxxiv. 35.

and a defence[1] upon the face of all knowledge. This is no doubt the meaning of the veil of Isis. This is the reason why so much of the ancient belief is wrapped up in symbolism, and why the ancient pictures are so full of symbols, for in them an initiate could tell at a glance how much the artist knew of the inner mysteries; for example, one often sees the ornamental broken pavement in ancient pictures. This was one of the many hints to look well into the picture and ponder much, for it represented not historical fact but mystic truth. The almond-shaped aura or *vesica piscis* was used in much the same way. Many pictures of the Ascension of Christ and of the Assumption of the Virgin contain the *vesica piscis* to show that if you did not believe these events to be historically true yet they are deep truths relating to the spirit and soul of every man—that the spirit and soul do ascend when their labours are done. The architects, too, were versed in these hidden truths, so that we may truly say that our great cathedrals and churches represent the sum-total of all the architect knew. They are really "frozen religion." The ordinary person sees a great and stately edifice but the initiate sees worlds on worlds unfold.

Black to us of the West is merely the sombre colour of mourning, a sign that our lives have been bereft of the joy of the presence of a loved one. It is perhaps the most depressing of all colours, physically, mentally, and morally, and surely if people believed

[1] Isaiah iv. 5.

in their religion they would never wear such a colour ; but unfortunately few people have the courage to go against custom, and to openly rejoice that their loved ones are in a better land. We may remember how the Lady Olivia's grief was reproved by the Clown in *Twelfth Night* :—

Clown : Good madonna, why mournest thou ?

Olivia : Good fool, for my brother's death.

Clown : I think his soul is in hell, madonna.

Olivia : I know his soul is in heaven, fool.

Clown : The more fool you, madonna, to mourn for your brother's soul being in heaven.

Of course black used with other colours often gives beautiful effects and throws these colours into relief. It is a most useful decorative colour when used in moderation, but when totally unrelieved, it is an abomination. By shutting out the light rays of the sun it lays the whole system open to disease. In the human aura it is evidence of the deepest depths of human wickedness.

Black in its lowest symbolism means this wickedness and foulness, and hatred of the light of the healing sun. The black angels are the evil angels. Black magic was occult art used for selfish purposes and very often requiring blood sacrifice, even of human blood, in the performing of it.

4

CHAPTER IX

THE OLD LANGUAGE OF BROWN AND GREY

> "Beauty is never lost,
> God's colours are all fast."—WHITTIER.

WE next consider the colour brown—the symbol of autumn and decay. The autumn may indeed be a beautiful season of mellow fruitfulness, and the rich red-brown hues may delight us, but for all this, the brown is a sign that the life is surely, though gently, passing away from the leaves. Yet because the tree does not die merely because the leaves perish, brown takes on the meaning of the still quietness that is necessary before the next period of effort. We have the expression "to be in a brown study," that is, in a calm state of mind, oblivious to external facts and objects for the time being, yet really working out some deep problem that has to be solved before physical effort is of any value. There is a softness and gentleness about brown which calms our restless minds.

Browns and other sombre "useful" colours are usually tabooed by healers because they tend to depression. If rest is needed, this is better given by blues and purples since they are quietening in effect. In ordinary household decoration, golden browns may be used with the most restful and helpful effect.

In the human aura, however, the presence of much brown indicates an unprogressed character—one who needs to make his life more spiritual.

Grey eyes are considered by many the best for expressing tenderness and sadness, but as a rule grey denotes what is hard and unfeeling. Still there are such a number of shades of grey that probably this last meaning is only appropriate to the shades having much blue in them.

Tennyson writes :—

> " Break, break, break,
>   On thy cold *grey* stones, O sea,
>   And I would that my tongue could utter
>   The thoughts that arise in me."

Kingsley writes :—

> " 'Tis the hard *grey* weather
>   Breeds hard Englishmen.
>
> .   .   .   .   .   .
>
>   Sends our English hearts of oak
>   Seaward round the world."

W. S. Cary, in " Heraclitus," writes :—

" They told me, Heraclitus, they told me you were dead ;
  They brought me bitter news to bear, and bitter tears to
      shed.
  I wept as I remembered how often you and I
  Had tired the sun with talking and sent him down the sky.

And now that thou art lying, my dear old Carian guest,
A handful of *grey* ashes, long, long ago at rest,
Still are thy pleasant voices, thy nightingales awake,
For Death, he taketh all away, but them he cannot take."

W. E. Henley, in his " Song of the Sword," sings :—

> " Follow, O follow me,
> Till the waste places
> All the *grey* globe over
> Ooze, as the honeycomb
> Drops, with the sweetness
> Distilled of my strength."

Again we must contrast this modern symbolism with the ancient. Grey was the union of black and white, and so partook of the symbolism of each. Christ in grey robes was not a cheerless Christ. His grey robes symbolised resurrection—the triumph of life over death; they symbolise the joy of white over the despair of black, of the joy of knowledge of future and everlasting life over the dark, inscrutable ways of apparent death.

The grey friars wore grey robes to portray Christ risen, still alive and working for the people of earth.

CHAPTER X

"Be thou the rainbow to the storms of life."—BYRON.

WE have come to the end of our survey of the inner meanings of separate colours, showing us how " The invisible things of God from the creation of the world are clearly seen, being understood by the things which are made." [1]

However, we should not properly complete our task if we did not consider the rainbow and the deep symbolic meaning attached to it. Since every ray gives out some great truth and blessing, the rainbow stood for all blessing, the sign of the presence of God's love. In Greece, Iris (who is sometimes regarded as the rainbow itself, or a goddess clothed with the rainbow, or dwelling in the rainbow, or making a rainbow path to earth) is the messenger of the gods. She is not mentioned in the *Odyssey* but very often in the *Iliad*. She has some of the functions of Hermes, but unlike Hermes has little or nothing to do with the pale realms of Pluto. She is generally looked upon as Juno's chief messenger, and confers blessings on those whom Juno loves.

[1] Romans i. 20.

In the *Æneid*, book iv., we have a beautiful description of Iris coming to release the suffering soul of Dido, the luckless Queen of Carthage :—

> "Then Juno, pitying her agony
>   Of lingering death, sent Iris down with speed
>   Her struggling soul from clinging limbs to free.
>
>   .   .   .   .
>
> So down to earth came Iris from on high
>   On saffron wings all glittering with the dew.
> A thousand tints against the sunlit sky
>   She flashed from out her rainbow as she flew."

The Scandinavians believed that on the rainbow arch the souls of the heroes were able to march in triumph to the great wassail in Valhalla. Curiously enough this rainbow is spoken of as "treble-hued." It would be interesting to know which three main colours of the rainbow they thought of.

" Over all swept the magnificent arch of Bifröst,[1] the treble-hued rainbow, and Odin turned and said : 'See, children, how Bifröst bids us climb yet higher, humbly to learn of the holy Nornir (the Fates) and drink in wisdom from the fountain of Urd (Norn of the Past). Let us mount and ride.' And the glorious procession took its way across the plain to the luminous trembling end of the bridge, where golden-toothed Heimdal (the sleepless guardian of Bifröst) stood on guard. With a smile of welcome he threw open the gate, and they swept proudly on, singing a song of joyous thanksgiving for the beauty and peace of all around them ; but, when great Thor would have set his foot on the bridge, Heimdal barred the way with his spear." [2]

---

[1] Bif-rost—the wave-rest, *i.e.* the resting place of the waves.

[2] *Asgard.* K. F. Boult.

So of all the gods Thor might not tread the rainbow; still, he was allowed to make his journey into the council of the gods by other paths.

The rainbow is said to have been given to Noah as a sign that there should be no more flood or no more sea of trouble, for the sea or the salt water stands mystically for the troubles, the trials, and the suffering which the soul has to surmount before it receives blessing and peace. How this makes us think of the meaning of Bifröst. The promise that there shall be no more sea does not stand for the drying-up of actual oceans but is a promise given to every true navigator of the soul—such as Noah was—if only the ark or soul is constructed according to divine instructions and has its little window above into which light may shine.

In the "Kalevala," Wainomoinem builds a magic boat, but forgets the last three words of his enchantment, and so he cannot complete the boat. He journeys over the whole world to find these words, and when he does eventually find them he finishes the boat and gives it as a dowry to the Maid of Beauty :—

> "Sitting on the arch of heaven
> On the bow of many colours."

Among the Peruvians the rainbow was worshipped under the name of Chucychu.

Ezekiel[1] sees the rainbow beautiful and bright around his vision of God and the Cherubim. St John[2] also has a vision of Christ manifesting within a rainbow glory.

[1] Ezekiel i. 28.   [2] Revelation iv. 3.

We should naturally expect from the above that the opal should have much the same meaning as the rainbow. We certainly do find that in the East it was considered a most sacred stone, and it was said to contain the Spirit of Truth.

The Greeks were probably responsible for our belief that it brings ill-luck in love affairs; but we must remember that they considered it capable of giving the gift of prophecy, provided that the gift was used for the benefit of others. If this was not so, then bad fortune came to the seer.

Joseph's coat of many colours has been said to have been a sign of all-blessing, but we must remember that there is considerable doubt concerning the context of this passage. Still we do know that in many nations certain variously coloured garments have been considered garments of honour. Thus the ancient Irish bards had robes striped with the following colours as a sign of their noble and honourable calling—white, blue, green, black, and red.

Modern symbolism speaks in very beautiful language of the fact that the seven rays of the spectrum give white light, but we must remember that this symbolism is essentially modern. Thus, as I have said previously, white represents unity; while to the ancients, yellow, the sun colour, was the colour of unity. The seven rays have been likened to the seven gifts of the Holy Spirit, and sometimes they are likened to the Elohim.

In the spectrum we have three main rays, sometimes given as red, yellow, and blue, and sometimes as red, green, and blue. These are said mystically to stand for the Trinity or God in Three—that is, God in manifestation; while the white ray would represent God in Unity or the One Supreme Cause—God Unmanifest—God ever changeless.

Sometimes the seven rays are likened to the various ways and methods of approach to spiritual vision, for few people receive this vision in the same way or under the same conditions. Some people receive inspiration through work, others in quiet meditation, or by concentrating their energies on some great truth. Thus the Zoroastrians and Parsees have concentrated on the virtue of Purity, and they realise that all that is unclean, whether of the body or of the soul, is forever separate from God. This is a great and basic truth that must be enshrined in the heart of every worshipper:—

" Blessed are the pure in heart : for they shall see God "

—a wonderful promise, hardly to be comprehended except by the saints, the seers, and the exalted ones.

Then the Buddhists lay stress on the Brotherhood of Man, and so charity and the virtue of giving willingly and freely has been exalted to one of supreme importance in India.

The Christians lay stress on the Love of God—the highest conception so far; but one that must include the other truths or it becomes degraded and debasing, as in the belief of the person who holds that the more wickedly he lives, the more God will have to forgive, and therefore the more love God will have for him.

So all Truths are necessary in order to form the white ray.   As James Russell Lowell says :—

"God sends His teachers into every land,
  To every clime and every race of men,
  With revelation fitted for their growth
  And shape of mind, nor gives the realm of Truth
  Into the keeping of one single race.

  .   .   .   .

  All nations have their message from on high,
  Each the Messiah of some central thought
  For the fulfilment and delight of man ;
  One has to teach that Labour is divine,
  Another Freedom and another Mind ;
  And all, that God is open-eyed and just,
  The happy centre and calm heart of all."

This wonderful study of symbolism sheds new light on many old customs and myths. From it, we are able to penetrate to the heart of things, and to see that every nation has aspired earnestly to understand the universe, and to realise that the Creator is manifest in His works.

Unfortunately the modern world in its haste has for many generations cast aside this desire to know more deeply these inner truths.   The Puritan saw that symbolism had degenerated into image-worship and into corrupt and unworthy practices, and so his mission was to destroy this dragon of false priests and to give simplicity and reality.   Almost too well he seems to the artist-minds to have done his work, but we must remember that it was an age of " No compromise."

Now, however, there seem to be signs all over the world that people would once again love to have these beautiful symbols, for just as the mathematician can reach greater truths by means of his symbols, so the mystic by his can attain to the highest realms of ecstasy. He becomes one of the uplifting forces of the world; one who gives light. His eyes and face reveal the inward light, and so he becomes a star. Mere knowledge, mere intellect, without the inner vision, never makes the star soul—" He whose face gives no light can never become a star." To such a one the object can never enslave. He has become, as the Hindoos say, " A King of the Zodiac "; that is, he has learnt all his lessons, journeyed through the twelve great constellations, performed his appointed labours, and is able to receive the great reward. What is the great reward? To see the spiritual significance burn through from all the objects of Nature and so to obtain communion with the Maker, and thus enter into the golden yellow petals of the Eternal Rose.

You ask me lastly why I think it is that the nations should agree so well in choosing the inner meanings of colours. It seems to me that in olden times the gift of being able to see the human aura was one well known to the prophets and seers. Now, once a person has this gift it is very easy to connect the type of person exhaling the aura with particular qualities. When another aura is seen containing one of the same colours the quality it shows would ever after be connected with that colour, and so there would grow up a colour symbolism differing little all over the world. Many of the most successful colour healers of to-day see the human aura, and according to the beauty of the colours they see the beauty of the Mind, and according to the lack of beautiful coloration they see illness and wrong-doing. Still it must be borne in mind that the wrong-doer even in health cannot attain so beautiful or refined an aura as the good man. In sickness the colours of the latter are greyish in value, whereas the colours of the evil man are muddy-looking.

It is indeed a great subject, proving that the physicians of the future must minister to the soul as well as the body. The world awaits them.

APPENDICES

APPENDIX I

SCHOOLS OF COLOUR (p. 25)

In these ancient schools of colour the students of seership concentrated for, sometimes, years on the truths coming to them from a given colour. Of the Persian Sufis there are said to have been four colours :—

1. Gold School.—Where all the beauty and majesty of the inner symbolism of the sun colour was to glorify their souls.
2. Green School.—Where they learnt of immortality, and the need of ever serving the Maker.
3. Black School.—Where they pondered on the mysteries of God and learnt wisdom thereby.
4. White School.—Where as full initiates they knew the joy of God.

There have also been rosaries of symbolic colours. Roses and prayers seem to have some connection in nearly all great religions, hence the colour of the rose was to denote a prayer or deep desire for the quality symbolised by the rose.

APPENDIX II

THE COLOURS OF THE PLANETS (p. 25)

THIS is a subject on which research gives variable results. In recent years Mr. Alan Leo, perhaps the greatest modern exponent of astrology, assigned the following colours to the planets :—

Sun	.	.	.	orange
Moon	.	.	.	violet
Mercury	.	.	.	yellow
Venus	.	.	.	blue
Mars	.	.	.	red
Jupiter	.	.	.	indigo
Saturn	.	.	.	green

A list perhaps more in harmony with the ancient beliefs is the one given below :—

Sun	.	yellow or gold
Moon	.	white or silver
Mercury	.	green
Venus	.	blue (turquoise or lapis lazuli)
Mars	.	red
Jupiter	.	purple (or lapis lazuli)
Saturn	.	black (sometimes black with orange flecks).

Saturn, it may be said, is the planet of mystery and the mysterious ways of God.   He is like the god Chronos or the Angel Oriphel ; he makes the person wait till his appointed hour before gifts are given.   Still, as he often, by means of waiting and suffering, causes the person to develop some of the very highest gifts, he is sometimes given the yellow flecks.

Minnie Theobald, in an explanation of a Passion play entitled *The Descent of the Light Spark*, writes on the colours worn by the Planets in her play.   I quote at some length :—

" These seven principles are represented in my drama as the seven planets, which in the ancient mode of consciousness typified different modes of consciousness and substance. . . . Neptune and Uranus are the two planets of regeneration and rebirth, they are connected with cosmic consciousness ; and so in the colour scheme either iridescence or all colour must be present to indicate their connection with wholeness. . . . Red typifies life and consciousness, and suggests the power of the Father, the Lord of Fire, reappearing in the lower worlds. Blue indicates the mother element or the substance into which life enters ; yellow stands for the personality or child. *Colour is language; any planet may be represented by any colour;* it depends upon the particular activity of the particular planetary spirit to be portrayed. In this drama Mercury or Memory, the messenger between Time and Eternity, wears red, for he is carrying life and consciousness down to the cross of matter. He is the representative in the lower regions of the Light Spark ; he is the flame hidden within each one of us, giving us memory of our divine origin. Next comes Venus, our fundamental soul-substance, the medium between the ego and personal mind ; she is clad in blue. Jupiter, personal mind, follows next, clad in yellow. Then we have Mars. Our soul-substance, blue, has become mingled with personal mind, yellow, and so we get green. Red, cosmic life becomes green, personal life, for after the birth of the personal mind everything becomes reversed. Our personal life-current is the complementary mode of activity to the crucified cosmic life-current. This personal life and passion is the field of activity of Mars, and so shows his complementary colour, green. Finally, black or Saturn marks the limit of the fall. Here we have the negation of the life of Eternity, black or dense matter being the inversion of the pure white light of spirit."

This last quotation will show how modern mysticism uses colours.

APPENDIX III

CHROMATICS OF THE SKY. By J. S. DYASON (p. 4)

The following is a tabulation of his observations :—

Copper at sunset	presages	wind or rain.
Bright yellow	,,	wind.
Pale yellow	,,	wet.
Rosy sky	,,	fine.
Pale green	,,	wind or rain.
Indian red	,,	wind.
Grey in the morning	,,	fine.
Red	,,	wind or rain.
Dark blue	,,	wind.
Bright blue	,,	fine.
A high dawn	,,	wind.
A low dawn	,,	fine.

APPENDIX IV

YELLOW (p. 15)

YELLOW is still a non-canonical colour in the church. Blue is also non-canonical.

The five canonical colours are (1) white used at Easter, Christmas, Circumcision, and Epiphany ; (2) red at Exaltation and Invention of Cross, Pentecost, and Feasts of Martyrs ; (3) violet on Ash Wednesday, Lent, Septuagesima, Quinquagesima, and Advent ; (4) black on Good Friday ; (5) green on ordinary Sundays and week days.

APPENDIX V

COLOUR AND FORM (p. 4)

SINCE colour is vibration, it is easy to see that it must also give form. Some of the most beautiful designs in the world have been produced by vibration. In his great book on *Colour*, Babbit takes red, yellow, and blue and gives them the forms of the triangle, the hexagon, and the circle. The triangle has the sharpest corners, thus it is appropriate to the energising fiery red. The circle, with no corners, represents the calm indwelling blue ; and the yellow, which has energy and yet peace, partakes of the hexagon, which still has angles but yet approaches the shape of the circle.

APPENDIX VI (p. 4)

M. CAMILLE FLAMMARION has made many interesting experiments on the growth of plants under different coloured rays. In one experiment he took young lettuces from the same plot of ground, and all the same size. His results showed that—

Under red glass lettuce grows four times as quickly as in direct sunlight.

  ,, green   ,,   ,, slightly quicker than in sunlight.

  ,, blue   ,, becomes very stunted.

In another experiment he worked with Indian corn.

In sunlight   one plant grew to 25 inches.
Under red glass ,,   ,,   ,,   18 ,,
  ,, green   ,,   ,,   ,,   8 ,,
  ,, blue   ,,   ,,   ,,   6 ,,
Beans flourished under white and red glass.
  ,, perished   ,, green ,, blue ,,

From the above it seems that blue glass is bad for plants ; but this is not always so, as is seen from the experiments of General Pleasanton, where he grew the best grapes in his district by using alternate white and blue glass in his greenhouses. Babbit states that blue light develops germination of plants, while red and yellow develop animalculæ. Yellow rays cause carbon to deposit from the air, and so form the woody fibre of plants. Red and yellow cause seeding and fruitage.